Billy Parker

Business start up mistakes

How to avoid common mistakes when
starting a business

First published by Nonsoul Publications 2022

Copyright © 2022 by Billy Parker

First edition

This book was professionally typeset on Reedsy
Find out more at reedsy.com

Table of Contents

- Not knowing your target audience

- Not writing a business plan

- Not employing help

INTRODUCTION

Botches are many times no in the public eye. We're told

to conceal errors or fault them on others, giving our best

for isolated ourselves from the dreadful weight of

accomplishing something wrong.

A great many people don't begin a business since they're reluctant to commit errors. In any case, here's the mystery: business botches don't stop your energy, they assist you with sorting out a superior way.

One of the most amazing certainty building techniques is regarding your missteps as opportunities for growth. Furthermore, in the realm of business venture, you will commit a great deal of errors. You can't stay away from them.

Luckily, you can anticipate some of them. This book will walk you through a few normal mix-ups, and ways to stay away from business disappointment.

NOT FOCUSING ON CASH FLOW AND PROFIT

One monetary slip-up business visionaries make is not focusing on income and benefits. Odds are good that your assets are in deals, promoting, or tech. Yet, it is basically impossible that a bootstrapped business can prevail without an organizer being totally on top of funds.

In the event that you ask any carefully prepared business visionary what the main expertise in maintaining a business is, they'll say it's math. A considerable lot of them start their business as a side interest and don't give as much consideration to the numbers as they ought to.

Business math works just to perceive how productive your business can be. Utilize this equation: Benefit = Demand x (Revenue - Expenses).

Furthermore, there are a great deal of costs to represent. As per an examination, private ventures spend a normal of $40,000 in their most memorable entire year of business. This is spent on the accompanying things:

We should separate the benefit recipe above. Expect there are 20,000 individuals looking for your item online each month. In the event that you can place yourself before even 50% of those individuals, that is 10,000 expected purchasers.

Assuming you convert at the normal of somewhere in the range of 1% and 2%, that is 100-200 deals. In the event that your typical request esteem is $100 and you have a net overall revenue of 30%, your benefit will be anything somewhere in the range of $3,000 and $6,000 each month.

Obviously, these are truly best guesses. Yet, anything that you get into, assuming you've figured it out, you understand what you're in for. Stay away from this normal mix-up by monitoring your possible benefits and income utilizing the above recipe.

The most effective methods to Fix Cash Flow Problems in a Small Business includes:

MAKE A CASH FLOW BUDGET

An income spending plan or conjecture is a gauge of how much cash you hope to see streaming all through your business during a particular time frame. By making this, you'll have the option to see which months you can hope to see a money deficiency, and which months you can anticipate an excess. You'll likewise have the option to find out about how much money your business will expect over the course of the following year or so to get by.

An income conjecture is likewise an extraordinary asset to assist you with settling on significant choices, for example, when to make a capital use, or the choice about whether to cut a cost.

MAKE IT EASIER TO GET PAID

Invoicing clients and trusting that those solicitations will get compensated can make an income bad dream. For organizations with income hardships, getting compensated rapidly is significant.

In the event that you don't as of now make it simple for clients to pay you, now is the ideal time to begin. Attempt a web based invoicing arrangement, as FreshBooks, that makes it simple to send solicitations and get compensated all on the web. That, however you can naturally send past due receipt notification to give clients a little update that you anticipate brief installment.

Besides, assuming you have a client that you charge a similar sum to month to month, as on a retainer or membership premise, you can likewise set up auto-charging to naturally charge their Mastercard month to month. Find arrangements that make it more straightforward to get compensated so you can invest less energy trusting that the money will hit your ledger.

CUT EXPENSES

In the event that you wind up continually coming up short with regards to cash, it very well may be an ideal opportunity to really investigate your costs. Costs can expand crazy when you're not focusing.

Begin by plunking down and checking out by any means of your decent costs. What can be cut? Are there expenses that you can decrease without an enormous business influence? Find those costs and perceive how eliminating them will influence your income financial plan.

ACCESS TO CASH

Indeed, even with the most cautious preparation, there will be times when clients don't pay and you end up in a tight income spot. To abstain from overreacting, you'll require a contingency plan: either a money save, or admittance to an advance or credit extension. Acquiring cash isn't intended to address your standard, continuous income issues, however it's great to know it's there for you to utilize infrequently when things don't go according to plan.

NOT ASSESSING YOUR BUSINESS IDEAS

Perhaps of the greatest error you can make while beginning another business is not doing statistical surveying. You need to find out about the opposition and comprehend how you can separate yourself from them. Rivalry can be other independent ventures conveying similar items as you, or it tends to be market monsters like Amazon and Walmart.

In some cases business visionaries plunge into a specialty market without deciding whether it's a solid match or not. There are situations where a specialty has low interest and an excess of laid out rivalry. Assuming that is the situation, you probably shouldn't fabricate a business around it.

To comprehend the market scene, you'll have to do some exploration. Track down your specialty's rivals and check out:

- Number of online surveys

- Social commitment

- Writing for a blog propensities

- Press inclusion

- Site improvement (SEO) rankings

You'll likewise need to assess whether the market is only a pattern or on the other hand on the off chance that it's a manageable class you can grow a presence in over the long haul.

How would you recognize and rule a business specialty market?

A business specialty is a particular or centered region of a more extensive market that your business serves explicitly. As per Charlene Walters, business and marking guide and creator of Own Your Other, finding a specialty separates your business from the opposition and permits you to succeed in your area.

Business people ought to consider a couple of key purchaser components while attempting to recognize and rule a specialty market. Search for the accompanying attributes in your potential market crowd:

1. Effectively recognizable clients: Potential clients who are not difficult to see are a sign of an extraordinary business spccialty. Jerry Rackley, head of promoting at Host Bridge Technology, said that it ought to be not difficult to recognize

who might work with you in view of a bunch of dependable qualities. "In the event that you can't place your ideal clients into a recognizable fragment, your marketable strategy is an off limits."

2. Effectively open clients: For a business specialty to be productive, your potential clients should be open, and getting to them should be reasonable, Rackley said. Any other way, your good thought will be down and out. "For instance, I could foster an optimal answer for roaming goat herders in Outer Mongolia, yet I have absolutely not a chance of contacting them with data about my answer," Rackley said. "Absence of openness is likewise a strategy off limits."

3. An undeserved or dismissed market: Many business sectors become over saturated with private ventures or new companies anxious to get in on the activity. Be that as it may, for a business specialty to truly stick out, it ought to help an undeserved or even ignored portion, said Cody McCain, boss visionary official at WircFuseMedia and a large group of the efficiency webcast Mind Hack. "In my encounters with facilitating organizations, there are frequently undeserved or totally disregarded markets, as well as business sectors that are inadequately served," McCain made sense of. McCain proposes exploring these business sectors in your industry as possible specialties. "For instance, in web facilitating, you can utilize Google Analytics and Google Ads to

find look through that are not returning outcomes to find markets or gatherings whose necessities are not being met. One more method for finding your specialty is to look through shopper appraisals files and locales to find regions with unfortunate client support.

·A huge expected market: For your business to be beneficial, your market and specialty should be enormous enough that you can bring in cash selling your items and administrations. "As well as distinguishing and getting to possible clients, there must be enough of them," Rackley said. "The expected market for any business should have the size and mass to warrant the venture to enter that market." He gave the case of "an extraordinary answer for any human who has at any point strolled on the outer layer of the moon." While it very well may be not difficult to recognize and try and get to moon walkers, presently, there simply aren't enough of them to qualify this as an incredible business specialty. A little pool of potential clients implies next to zero development potential, one more basic quality of a productive business specialty.

NOT KNOWING YOUR TARGET AUDIENCE

Doing quality examination comes in two sections: tracking down item thoughts and knowing your clients. The precarious thing here is that you can have clients and afterward construct an item, however having an item and afterward chase after customers is truly challenging.

The vast majority of the tried and true way of thinking says to take a gander at numbers and examination while investigating a specialty, and that is totally important. Be that as it may, another basic step most business people miss is finding an ideal client and building a client profile.

"The best methodology a bootstrapping business visionary can take to comprehend their clients is to handle predictable discussions with them," makes sense of Adrienne Barnes, Founder of Best Buyer Persona. "Establish a climate where each individual who associates with the client is gathering information to realize them better."

At the point when you know who your clients are, the means by which they act, and why they act the manner in which they do, you'll have the option to serve them such that addresses their issues. Adrienne Barnes

Regardless of whether your specialty has adequate interest and a decent determination of items, without knowing your ideal client, it will be significantly more enthusiastically to sell.

Assuming you dig sufficiently profound, you will find that specialties encapsulate specialties. The more you can focus on, the better, since it will be simpler to relate to your clients' necessities.

You want to make some deal, yet attempting to offer to everybody and everything, with no objective market, no specialty marking, and no voice is only a catastrophe waiting to happen. Additionally, attempting to do a lot of excessively fast, can extended you very far.

Step by step instructions to Define Your Target Audience: 6 Questions to Ask

Sorting out your main interest group isn't overly complicated. It boils down to a couple of straightforward inquiries.

Six really, to be accurate.

Go through every one of the inquiries beneath and you'll know the specific crowd you are focusing on.

1. Who Are They?

While contemplating who may be in your crowd, you should consider who are individuals who relate to your image.

One method for finding out is to screen who follows, likes, offers, and remarks on your posts on friendly locales like Facebook, LinkedIn, YouTube, and Instagram.

In the event that somebody will draw in with you, odds are they are your objective.

Much of the time, your ideal crowd may not be latent via web-based entertainment, but rather purchase from your organization every now and again or pursue your administrations.

Indeed, the people who purchased from you just once should be viewed as a piece of your ideal interest group, as somebody who purchased once could purchase once more.

It is useless to put forth an extraordinary attempt to sell in the event that you don't put forth a comparable attempt to keep the clients you have proactively acquired.

Clients like to feel extraordinary, and for that reason the post-deals process is so significant. Your relationship with the client should stay even after the buy is finished.

2. What Are Their Biggest Difficulties, Problems, or Desires?

What is cool, fascinating, and great for you probably won't be for the client.

Try not to think about yourself when now is the right time to characterize the troubles, issues, and wants of your ideal interest group. Come at the situation from their perspective.

Try not to make offers in view of your thought process. Make them as per research grounded in information, past encounters, and examination of your possible clients' way of behaving.

Comprehend the best hardships your crowd countenances to attempt to assist with tackling them.

3. Where Do They Look for Information Online?

Everybody needs data.

Consistently we are immersed with lots of data, yet when you really want it the most, where do you go to track down replies?

Distinguish the correspondence channels generally fitting to your interest group and attempt to converse with them utilizing a particular language from their universe.

For instance, I understand where my listeners might be coming from peruses showcasing websites and invests a ton of energy in friendly locales like YouTube and LinkedIn consuming data.

4. What Real Benefit Do You Offer?

Everybody needs answers for their concerns and to make their lives more straightforward. This is an aggregate longing and it's the same for your ideal interest group.

Contemplate your item and the issue it settles. What advantages does your item or administration offer? How might it take care of those issues? What is the fundamental worth proposition?

With such a lot of rivalry, you should attempt to track down your upper hand in your specialty and consistently attempt to work on your item, offering a bonus that others don't. For instance, better client care, a free device, or a free time for testing.

5. What Draws Their Attention Negatively?

Being hopeful aides a ton, however contemplating the negatives can likewise help, particularly when we discuss interest groups.

Better than thinking about what your crowd needs, contemplate what they certainly don't need and what they stay away from.

With this strong data close by, you might have more opportunities to enrapture your possible clients.

Keeping away from what they consider negative is the initial step to acquire their endorsement. From that point onward, you just have to apply different procedures to do proficient advertising.

6. Who Do They Trust?

Trust is everything to your ideal interest group. Nobody buys an item or administration from an organization they don't have the foggiest idea or trust.

To this end audits on Amazon are perused thus significant for venders. They realize it constructs trust; it's likewise assisted Amazon with turning into a trillion-dollar organization.

Despite the fact that this is the last inquiry, it is one of the most significant.

The standing of your organization is significant. Dealing with the relationship with your clients is fundamental as they spread data about your image on the web and to their loved ones.

In the event that you get great surveys, have positive remarks, and gather an extraordinary standing, clients will be more persuaded to purchase from you.

NOT WRITING A BUSINESS PLAN

Composing a strategy is a significant piece of making a manageable business and standing apart from the opposition. An essential marketable strategy makes energy, and that implies that since you have an unmistakable and investigated thought, you are motivated to succeed.

However, numerous new business visionaries start their endeavor without pondering the higher perspective. They then, at that point, have no comprehension of the market, monetary, plan of action, or strategies, and that absence of understanding can cost time, cash, and exertion when things turn out badly. They likewise don't have a statement of purpose to hold on when circumstances become difficult.

Stay away from this normal misstep by making a strategy to assist with distinguishing the questions and spot the holes you really want to fill. Do you have to physically work with a 3PL or transport? How might you make items? Who are you offering to?

Each item you make ought to relate back to your field-tested strategy. This assists you with keeping focused to address your business' issues and objectives   and fabricate one that doesn't fall flat.

Instructions to compose a strategy bit by bit

1. Chief rundown

The chief rundown is an outline of your business and your arrangements. It starts things out in your arrangement and is preferably only one to two pages. However, the vast majority compose it last.

Preferably, the leader rundown can go about as an independent report that covers the features of your definite arrangement. As a matter of fact, it's exceptionally normal for financial backers to request just the leader outline when they are assessing your business. In the event that they like what they find in the chief rundown, they'll frequently circle back to a solicitation for a total arrangement, a pitch show, and more top to bottom financials.

Your leader outline ought to incorporate a synopsis of the issue you are tackling, a portrayal of your item or administration, an outline of your objective market, a concise depiction of your group, a rundown of your financials, and your subsidizing necessities (in the event that you are fund-raising).

Dive more deeply into composing a viable chief outline.

2. Items and administrations

The items and administrations part of your strategy is where the genuine meat of your arrangement resides. It incorporates data about the issue that you're addressing, your answer, and how your item or administration squeezes into the current cutthroat scene.

Begin the items and administrations part by depicting the issue that you are settling for your clients and what your answer is. This is a depiction of your item or administration.

Then, you ought to frame your opposition. Who else is giving arrangements that attempt to settle your clients' trouble spots? What are your upper hands over different organizations?

In the event that you end up enjoying any cutthroat benefits, for example, explicit licensed innovation or licenses that safeguard your item — this section is an extraordinary spot to discuss those things.

At last, audit your achievements and measurements. This is an outline of the following stages that you want to achieve to prepare your item or administration to sell, with deadlines. Assuming you've proactively accomplished a few key achievements, like handling a critical client or taking on pre-orders, examine that here.

3. Market investigation

This part is where you will grandstand all of the data about your possible clients. You'll cover your objective market as well as data about the development of your market and your industry.

To begin with, depict your objective market. Your objective market is the gathering that you anticipate offering to. Attempt to be essentially as unambiguous as could be expected. With a strong objective market, making a deals and promoting plan that will arrive at your customers will be simpler.

Then, give any market examination and statistical surveying that you have. You'll need to make sense of how your market is developing after some time and furthermore make sense of how your business is situated to exploit anticipated changes in your industry.

4. Advertising and deals

The showcasing and deals plan segment of your field-tested strategy subtleties how you intend to arrive at your objective market sections, how you anticipate offering to those target markets, what your estimating plan, and kinds of exercises and organizations you really want to make your business a triumph.

A few organizations that disseminate their items and arrive at their clients through stores like Amazon.com,

Walmart, Target, supermarket chains, and other retail outlets ought to survey how this piece of their business functions. The arrangement ought to talk about the coordinated operations and expenses of getting items onto store racks and any potential obstacles that the business might need to survive.

The promoting and deals section of your field-tested strategy can likewise be a decent spot to incorporate a SWOT examination. This is simply discretionary yet can be an effective method for making sense of how your items and administrations are situated to manage cutthroat dangers and make the most of chances.

5. Organization association and supervisory group

Financial backers search for extraordinary groups notwithstanding good thoughts. Utilize this section to depict your ongoing group and who you want to enlist. You will likewise give a fast outline of your lawful design, area, and history in the event that you're as of now going.

Incorporate brief profiles that feature the significant encounters of each key colleague. It's significant here to present the defense for why the group is the right group to transform a thought into a reality. Do they have the right business experience and foundation? Have individuals from the group had enterprising triumphs previously?

Your organization outline ought to likewise incorporate a rundown of your organization's ongoing business structure. The most well-known business structures include:

- LLC
- C-corp
- S-corp
- Sole owner
- Association

Make certain to give a survey of how the business is possessed too. Does every colleague claim an equivalent piece of the business? How is proprietorship partitioned? Expected banks and financial backers will need to know the design of the business before they will think about a credit or venture.

6. Monetary projections

Last, yet absolutely not least, is your monetary arrangement section. This is many times what business people see as generally overwhelming, yet it doesn't need to be pretty much as scary as it appears. Business financials for most new companies are less convoluted than you suspect, and a business degree is surely not expected to fabricate a strong monetary conjecture. All things considered, on the off chance that you want extra assistance, there are a lot of devices and assets out there to assist you with building a strong monetary arrangement.

A normal monetary arrangement will include:

Deals and income projections

A month to month deals and income conjecture for the initial a year, and afterward yearly projections for the leftover three to five years. Three-year projections are commonly satisfactory, yet a few financial backers will demand a five-year gauge.

Benefit and misfortune explanation

A pay explanation, otherwise called the benefit and misfortune (or P&L), is where your numbers generally meet up and show on the off chance that you're creating a gain or assuming a misfortune.

Income proclamation

An income proclamation. While the pay articulation computes your benefits and misfortunes, the income

NOT EMPLOYING HELP

Doing it single-highhandedly is the primary way of thinking for some business people.

In financial matters, there is an idea of chance expense. Basically, whenever you decide to seek after any a single an open door, the "cost" of that to you is that your time is presently not free for different open doors. So the expense of a single open door is really every other open door you have.

Assuming you are bootstrapping your own business, odds are you did everything yourself. You set up the site, you dabbled with it, you transferred items, you composed all the item portrayals, you did all the promoting. A marvelous one-individual show.

The issue here is that while doing all that yourself is perfect, it's additionally amazingly tedious. This is time you could be utilizing somewhere else — enjoying it with your family, concocting novel thoughts, or building business connections, just to give some examples.

Humble assignments come in two assortments: vital and superfluous.

You need to attempt to mechanize however many important modest undertakings as could be allowed. This interaction will cost a touch of cash, yet the cerebral pain and despair you set aside commonly offsets the cash you'll spend. Furthermore, you can frequently find individuals that will readily do these undertakings (stock transferring, information section, and so on) for you for a sensible total.

Pointless modest errands need to go in peril. By pointless, I mean things like investing a lot of energy dabbling with your site's logo, tinkering with picture sizes, carefully describing the shade of a button, or some other minor change that presumably you alone have taken note.

A portion of the things referenced above can decidedly affect your changes. Yet, you'll just know once you have a ton of guests and deals to contrast it with. In the beginning phases of your business, you need to stay away from those things. Particularly since, following two hours of dabbling, you'll feel as you did a great deal of work, yet all things considered, your time might have been exceptional spent.

A business choice you'll need to make is in the event that you really want to recruit help. This could be a prime supporter or a consultant.

Luckily, you can anticipate some of them. This book will walk you through a few normal mix-ups, and ways to stay away from business disappointment.

* 9 7 9 8 8 4 6 7 3 2 7 0 4 *